Daphney Dollar & Friends

First Allowance

Written by Sharon M. Lewis

Illustrated by Mona M. Spencer

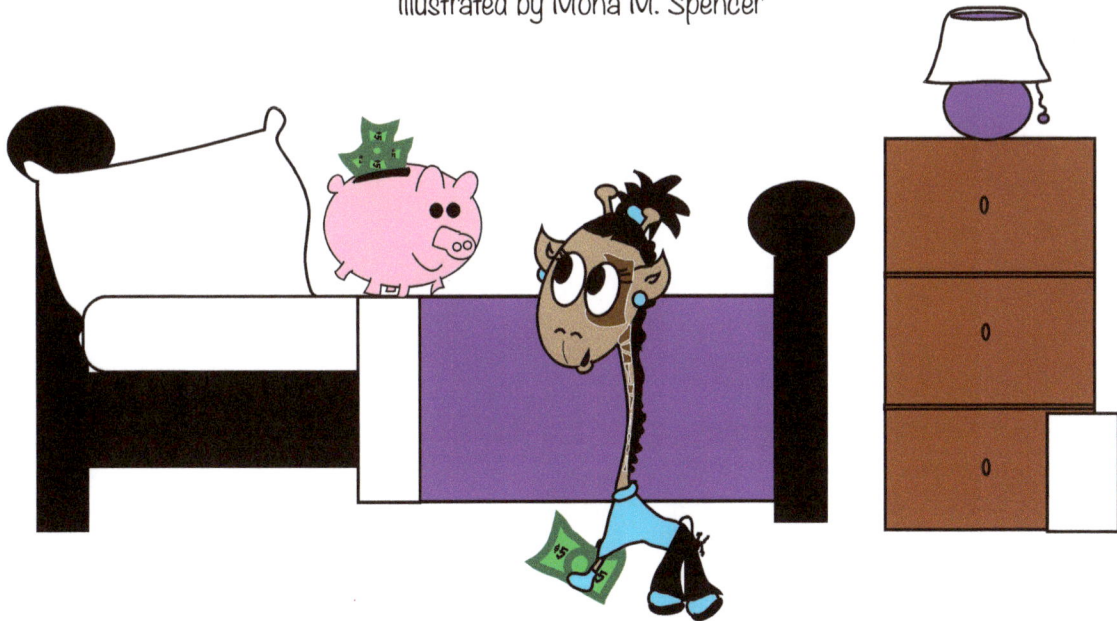

Daphney Dollar & Friends

I extend a special thanks to my husband Alvin and my children for being the light of my life. Thank you, my sister, Mona Spencer, for working tirelessly on the illustrations. I thank my siblings, my parents, and grandparents for all that they have done to make me the person that I am today. I love you all so much! Special thanks to all of my friends and acquaintances for their encouragement and feedback on this book. Thank you. Thank you. Thank you.

Daphney Dollar sits in her room. Her daddy's birthday is next month, and she wants to buy something really special for him. Daphney starts thinking of all the things she wants to buy for her daddy. Should she buy him a notebook? Should she buy him cologne? Should she buy him a tie?

Yes!! Yes!! A tie. Daddy wears plenty of ties to work. I think he likes new ties!

Daddy's birthday is September 19th and I want to buy him something nice!
Okay Daphney eat your breakfast and I will see what I can do.

Mrs. Dollar thinks about giving her $20. She realizes that Daphney is five years old now and she should start receiving a weekly allowance.

It seems appropriate to give Daphney $5 as she is five years old.
By giving Daphney an allowance, she can begin to save her money.

An allowance is a weekly dollar amount that parents give children. This gives children the chance to save money or spend their money on special gifts for their families or purchase special items for themselves.

I am giving you $5 every week and with each year that you grow older, your allowance goes up by $1. That is your raise.

✓ You get $5.00 a week.

✓ There is a $1.00 raise every year.

✓ By the end of every year your total savings will increase!

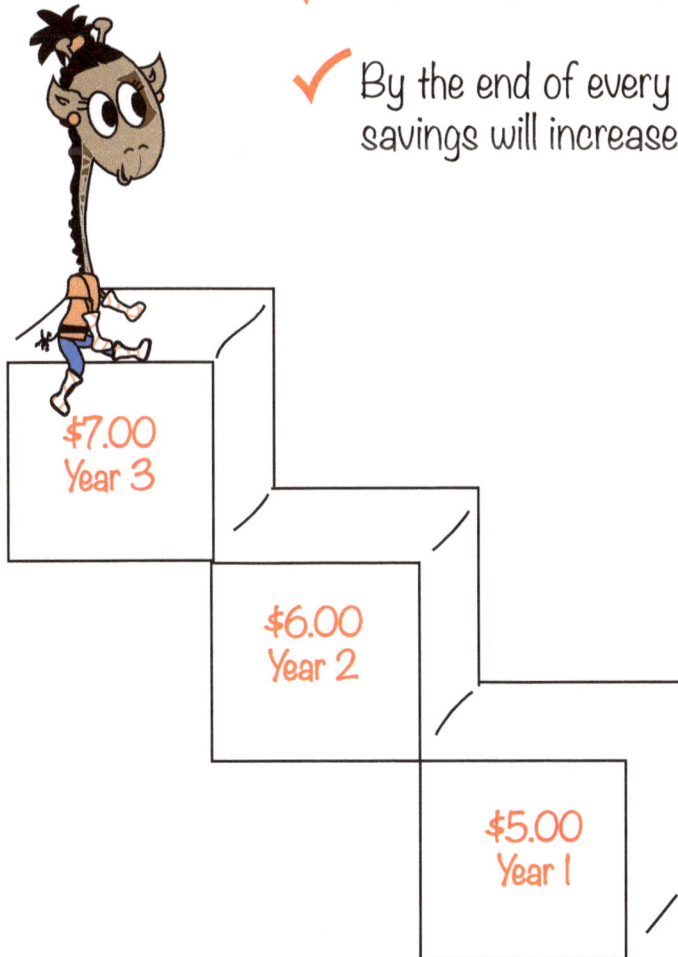

$7.00
Year 3

$6.00
Year 2

$5.00
Year 1

So when I turn 6, I receive $6 every week...and then when I turn 7, I receive $7. I am rich!!! Rich!! So rich!!

Ok, ok Daphney. You are not rich right now , but remember that it is never "how much you receive in allowance, it is how much you save." As you grow older, we can talk about ways to save your allowance.

Mommy, I am so happy. That means if you give me $5 every week for four weeks, I can save $20 when daddy's birthday comes around. This is enough for me to buy daddy's gift!!!

$5.00 Week #1

+ $5.00 Week #2

+ $5.00 Week #3

+ $5.00 Week #4

———————————

= $20.00

The End

www.ingramcontent.com/pod-product-compliance
Lightning Source LLC
Chambersburg PA
CBHW041600260326
41914CB00011B/1326